ignite your magic

a self-discovery journal

# ignite your magic

## A SELF-DISCOVERY JOURNAL

### Prompts and Exercises to Inspire Personal Growth

**Elena Lipson**

ROCKRIDGE
PRESS

For general information on our other products and services or to obtain technical support, please contact our Customer Care Department within the United States at (866) 744-2665, or outside the United States at (510) 253-0500.

Rockridge Press publishes its books in a variety of electronic and print formats. Some content that appears in print may not be available in electronic books, and vice versa.

TRADEMARKS: Rockridge Press and the Rockridge Press logo are trademarks or registered trademarks of Callisto Media Inc. and/or its affiliates, in the United States and other countries, and may not be used without written permission. All other trademarks are the property of their respective owners. Rockridge Press is not associated with any product or vendor mentioned in this book.

Interior Designer: Marietta Anastassatos
Cover Designer: Stephanie Mautone
Art Producer: Samantha Ulban
Editor: Carolyn Abate
Production Editor: Matthew Burnett
Production Manager: Riley Hoffman

All images used under license © Sergeypeterman/Creative Market and Shutterstock.
Author photography courtesy of Tiffany Brooks

Paperback ISBN: 978-1-63807-704-6
R0

This Journal Belongs to:

........................................................................................

"And above all, watch with glittering

eyes the whole world around you

because the greatest secrets are

always hidden in the most unlikely

places. Those who don't believe

in magic will never find it."

—ROALD DAHL

# Contents

Introduction  viii

**Get to Know Yourself (Again)**  3

**Have Compassion and Gratitude for Your Journey**  31

**See the World Anew**  57

**Light Your Creative Fire**  83

**Build Community That Sparks Joy**  109

**Nurture Your Magic and Watch It Grow**  137

**A Final Word**  165

Resources  166

References  167

# Introduction

**M**AGIC IS A PART OF ALL OF OUR LIVES. Whether it's observing the colors on the wings of a fluttering butterfly, watching puffy cloud animals drifting through the blue sky, or gazing at the shimmering sparkle of the ocean on a sunny day, we feel most alive when our senses of beauty, possibility, and awe are activated.

Each of us is born with our own magic in our lives. But as you grow up, take on new responsibilities, and integrate into adult society, it's easy to lose sight of what makes you feel most alive, and instead focus on the practical and mundane. In other words, you lose touch with your truest self—your magic.

From early on in my life, I've been fascinated by people, the choices we make, and the ways in which we relate to each other. It's no wonder that I landed in the world of personal development and leadership coaching. Even though my career started in sales and training in the corporate world, I currently own and operate my own coaching company, Source Strategies. Over the last two decades, I've had the opportunity to create self-care, personal growth, and intuitive strategy courses for individuals and groups.

Over the years, I've worked as a coach, speaker, writer, meditation guide, and retreat leader. I've studied the choices that people make, and how those choices create lives full of satisfaction, growth, and inspiration. I've guided thousands of clients to incorporate and embrace transformational personal habits and practices into their days so they can ignite that inner magic. I've collected lessons, tools, and resources and poured them into this journal for you. Inside you'll create tiny shifts that lead to a life of more meaning and purpose—and of course, one filled with your own special magic.

This book is divided into six parts. Each part focuses on a different theme, ranging from gratitude to personal courage. You will see a selection of unique prompts, exercises, and affirmations throughout each section. The journal prompts will help you thoughtfully reflect on your past, present, and future. The exercises will invite you to go beyond the journal pages and practice embodying the concepts within each section. This will help you use muscle memory to make and hold on to those changes in your life. Together, these elements will help you release what is no longer working for you, reclaim your authentic self, and (re)ignite your magic.

You can use this journal as a daily oracle practice, opening to any page and trusting that this is exactly what you need on that particular day. Or, if you prefer, you can start from section one, and let the journey build and unfold as you go. You can even get yourself a special "magic" pen that you use only for this journal, to add a layer of focus and intention.

Please remember that while a guided journal practice is a great way to work through complex feelings, any ongoing or debilitating feelings of anxiety or depression should be addressed by a medical professional. This book is not a replacement for a therapist, medication, or medical treatment. There is truly no shame in seeking help or treatment.

There is no one right way to experience this journal. The fact that you are reading these words right now means that you are exactly where you need to be, and you are investing time and energy in yourself. This self-care leads to realizations, awareness, and synchronicity in your life. I am celebrating you, and invite you to celebrate yourself right now.

Most importantly, I want you to know that the magic you are seeking is already within you. You don't have to go anywhere exotic or do anything that doesn't feel good or aligned to you in order to find it. I'm eager to show you the steps to create your own magic toolbox and how to access it whenever you need it to tap into your most authentic self. If you make the commitment to using this journal, you're also making a commitment to yourself. And each day you use it, you will begin to reclaim or rediscover your innate magic.

Your first step is to set your intention for how you want to show up for yourself throughout this new journal practice. This can be as simple as saying, "My intention is to show up with love and compassion," or "My intention is to have fun and stay positive, even when it feels difficult."

Your turn: "My intention is

"Magic is believing in yourself, if you can do that, you can make anything happen."

—JOHANN WOLFGANG VON GOETHE

# Get to Know Yourself (Again)

As you begin this journey, give yourself permission to momentarily let go of your busy adult self so that you can experience childlike joy, limitless creativity, and new possibilities. In this section, you'll find exercises and prompts that can help you slow down and become enchanted with ordinary moments, make room for magic in your life, and inspire those around you to do the same.

Because your brain is so efficient, it turns most of your repetitive actions into habits that you barely think about doing. This puts you in autopilot mode for much of those activities that you repeat throughout your day. One fun way you can experience more presence is to do the things you normally do, but in a slightly different way. For example, switching to the other hand when you brush your teeth.

Using your nondominant hand, in the lines below write out directions from your home to the market.

How did it feel?

When you feel like your spark is dimmed, it can usually be traced back to a way in which you're living that doesn't feel right, or feels misaligned. Make a list of at least five things in your home environment that you tolerate, but don't love or cherish, like a lamp you inherited and feel guilty about giving away. Then brainstorm how to improve the situation. It could be as simple as decluttering a messy drawer, or donating clothes that no longer fit or feel joyful when you wear them.

Have you ever noticed how much time children spend barefoot? It's like they instinctively know that staying connected to the earth is good for them.

Right now, get barefoot and go play outside for a few minutes—or more, if you dare. Even just standing on a patch of grass or earth can help you feel more connected.

As people age, they tend to get very serious and focus on life's responsibilities. One area that often gets sidelined is the magic of friendship. Yet studies show that fun, play, and laughter with friends can help heal the mind and body, and create more satisfaction regardless of one's circumstances.

Ask yourself: If I made time for fun with one or more friends, how would we spend an entire day together? Below, plan out a few ideas to make this happen; they can be as simple as a phone call or invitation to take a walk or get coffee or tea together.

As we get older, we tend to become more serious. This is unfortunate because laughter and joy decrease stress hormones, increase immune strength, and release endorphins. Get joyful with this exercise.

Inhale deeply and smile. Open your hands and spread your fingers, pointing them upward in a clapping position.

1. Inhale and exhale, then exclaim "I AM GRATEFUL!" Clap your hands three times—once for each word.

2. Repeat twice.

3. Inhale, lift your arms and face toward the sky, and as you exhale, say "YES!"

4. Repeat as many times as you like.

5. Place your left hand over your heart, your right hand over your belly, and laugh.

There is a near-infinite variety of online classes available. Whether you're interested in illustration, dance, or creative writing, for a few dollars and some time, you can infuse new energy into your life. The key here is to let your intuitive side, rather than your logical and practical side, help you decide on a class. If you can't quite figure it out, take a few slow, deep breaths, relax your shoulders, slow down, and answer the following question:

"What kinds of things am I doing when I feel the most 'myself?'"

One of the best ways to create magic in your life is to intentionally make time for what fills you up. This includes doing more of what feels good in your body, as well as what feels good mentally and emotionally. A great place to start is by making a list of feel-good activities, organized by how much time they take. The trick is to keep this list on hand and create sweet pockets of time with the intention of nourishing your spirit.

| GOOD (5–15 MINUTES) | BETTER (15–30 MINUTES) | BEST (60+ MINUTES) |
| --- | --- | --- |
| *Ex: Take a nap, prepare a healthy snack and sit to enjoy it* | *Ex: Work on a writing project, enjoy some tea, repot a plant, take a walk* | *Ex: Declutter the closet, meet with a friend for a hike* |

Before anyone told you how to spend your day, you simply followed your inner compass and did whatever felt fun moment by moment. This is the magic of childlike play. How can you add an element of this joyful activity to your life now? It could be as simple as blocking out a "playtime" hour (or more!) on your calendar at least once a week.

When you were little, what did you love to spend endless time doing? Write down your idea and use it as a jumping-off point for playtime. If you get stuck, consult with your inner eight-year-old for ideas.

One way to explore ideas for new things to try is to draw a circle with the phrase NEW THINGS in the middle, and then make lines away from the circle with as many ideas as you can think of. Don't be scared to get messy and wild, with circles in every direction! Challenge yourself to make at least ten circles.

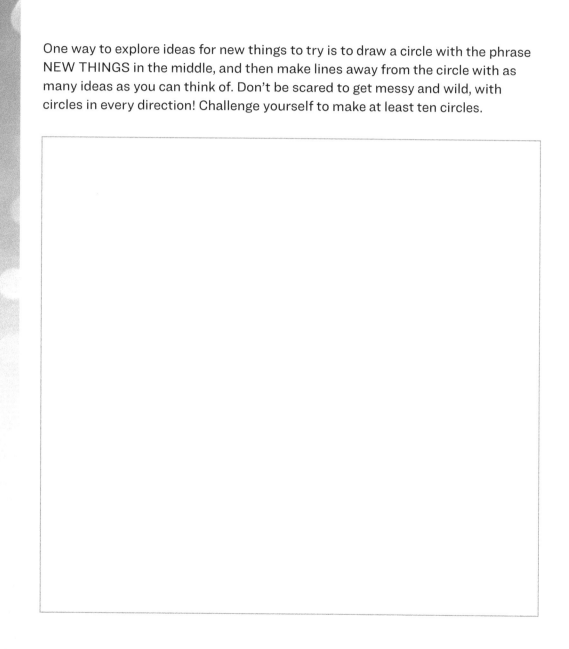

Now take a look at the ideas within each of your circles, even the crazy or silly ones. Do any of these ideas stand out? Take one of these ideas and write down one tiny step you can take to try one of these new things today.

Giving thoughtful and personal gifts can spark magic in our relationships. To explore new ways of giving and receiving in your life, consider the following questions: What is the best present I have ever received? What was it about this gift that made it so special to me?

_____

_____

_____

_____

_____

_____

What was the best present I have ever given? What was it about this gift that made it special for the recipient?

_____

_____

_____

_____

_____

_____

One of the ways you can express your authentic self is through your clothing choices. Think about the following statements and reflect on where you land.

- Do you feel like your clothing expresses your personal style?

- Is there anything that you'd like to change?

- What do you wear that makes you feel like the best version of you?

- How can you add some fun into your personal style?

Set aside a few hours to go through each item in your closet and decide whether you want to keep it (because it brings you joy), donate or sell it (so someone else can enjoy it), or ditch it (because it's beyond repair).

You were born with a unique way to express yourself, as one-of-a-kind as your fingerprint. As you got older, the adults around you began giving you their opinions, approval, and spoken and unspoken expectations. They did the best they could, but they were operating from their own limitations. Once we identify those limitations, we can begin to reclaim our own way of being, one that reflects who we truly are. How did others describe you when you were little? Do you agree with their description? Why or why not?

You don't have to wait until you hit a huge milestone to celebrate yourself and your accomplishments. In fact, the more you celebrate the tiny wins, the more wins, big and small, you will have to celebrate. This is all about intention, focusing on what you want more of, and being clear about what matters to you. With that in mind, what is one thing in your life that you can celebrate today? How will you celebrate? Do so, and make this a daily habit for one week.

Let's bust that myth that rest, play, and doing absolutely nothing are not permitted unless you have "earned" the right to them by first pushing yourself to exhaustion. In fact, studies show that time off actually enhances your creativity and ability to find new solutions to challenges both in life and at work.

Let's explore your relationship to "being busy." Do you feel like you have to earn time to relax? Be specific.

_____

_____

_____

_____

_____

How can you add more time for "doing nothing" throughout your day, week, and month? After you figure it out, don't forget to add it to your calendar.

_____

_____

_____

_____

_____

In our modern lives, people tend to work, life, and family commitments. We rarely make time for fun. Making time to play with your partner, friends, and children, and even pets, is a great way to boost your imagination and creativity, problem-solving skills, and emotional health. Being playful can mean many things—inviting friends or family for a game night, or dressing up in fancy clothes for dinner each Friday night. What are some ways you can add more play to your daily life?

One of the things that children do so well is daydream. Take some time to sit and daydream. This can be as simple as sitting outside and looking up at the clouds. Notice any resistance that comes up, or that inner voice telling you that you should be doing something. Set a timer, if that feels good. When you're done, come back and reflect on your experience, and any inspiration that you found during your daydreaming.

Gratitude and appreciation are powerful tools to tap into your inner magic. What are 10 things you can appreciate about yourself right at this moment?

1. ...........................................................................................................................................

2. ...........................................................................................................................................

3. ...........................................................................................................................................

4. ...........................................................................................................................................

5. ...........................................................................................................................................

6. ...........................................................................................................................................

7. ...........................................................................................................................................

8. ...........................................................................................................................................

9. ...........................................................................................................................................

10. ...........................................................................................................................................

Breathing with intention is a great way to bring awareness to your emotions. Right now, and anytime you want to feel more present to the magic of the moment, I invite you to practice what I call the "4 x 4 box breath."

Step one: Breathe in as you silently count to four, then hold for fourseconds.

Step two: Breathe out to the count of four, then hold for four seconds.

Step three: Repeat four to five times, at your own pace.

We all have things we want to do that we've never gotten around to—often simple things like taking a weekly walk along the beach, or spending a few minutes in the evening reading before you go to bed.

Write out two or three fun or nourishing ideas. They don't have to be time-intensive—they can take just 10 or 20 minutes to accomplish.

_____

_____

_____

_____

_____

Now that you've got a few ideas, think about why you've put them off for so long. Money, time, ability? What can you do now to change things, so that this time you actually act on these ideas?

_____

_____

_____

_____

_____

Take a slow walk outside, simply noticing all of the sounds you hear and the colors you see. Make this a walking meditation where you take in your full surroundings.

Instead of walking to get from point A to point B, slow down and ask yourself what you see, smell, and feel.

Afterward, write in your journal and reflect on the things you never stopped to notice before.

One of the things that makes childhood so magical is that you are doing so many things for the first time. Once the novelty of those "firsts" goes away, you can get bored and frustrated by the sameness of it all. That's why it's important to try new things. Just thinking about new ideas can bring that spark back into your life, such as new recipes, a new restaurant, or taking a new route to work. When was the last time you tried something new? How could you make more time to try something new again?

Take a nap. Whether you snuggle with a pet on the couch,
or head back into your comfy bed, set the alarm for
15-20 minutes and enjoy. Don't worry about actually falling
asleep. The act of laying down and resting is enough to give
your body and brain a much-needed reset.

Music is a source of joy and play, the backdrop to our lives. Just putting on a song that reminds you of a specific time in your life can transport you back to it. Think about the songs that make you smile, feel like dancing, and bring you joy.

Make a Magic Music Playlist of the songs you love. Anytime you think of a new song, or hear a song that you like, add it to the list. You can use any music service you prefer, like Spotify, Pandora, Apple Music, or others.

"The appearance of things changes

according to the emotions, and

thus we see magic and beauty

in them, while the magic and

beauty are really in ourselves."

—KAHLIL GIBRAN

Close your eyes, put your hand on your heart, and slowly repeat this three times: "The more I let myself play, the more I allow magic to flow my way."

"Gratitude makes sense of our past,

brings peace for today, and

creates a vision for tomorrow."

—MELODY BEATTIE

# Have Compassion and Gratitude for Your Journey

When you learn to trust yourself and your own inner power, you can trust that all of the pivots and detours of your life are taking you in the right direction—even if it doesn't feel like that at the moment. You can walk in daily intention and gratitude. In this section, we will explore the gifts and lessons of your past. By taking the time to seek out, notice, and acknowledge the things you're grateful for, you will start to see that even the unpleasant moments in your life have gifts and lessons for you.

It's important to remember that the way you see life is, in large part, a habit based on where you focus your attention. For now, I invite you to focus your attention on the good. Set a timer for five minutes and write only positive things about your life, your past, and yourself. Keep the pen moving until the five minutes are up.

Think about a time in the past year when you made a mistake at work or in a relationship. Maybe you missed a deadline on an important project, causing a delay for others, or maybe you forgot to acknowledge someone's birthday. Mistakes and failures can feel stressful, but they are normal. They teach us important lessons about life and about ourselves.

Write about a mistake or failure from the past year that still weighs on your mind and heart, and at least one lesson you can learn from it.

It's difficult to find any logic or reason when dealing with something unpleasant or difficult in your life. But you always have a choice about where to focus your attention. Writing a gratitude list helps you tune in to what is already good about your life. It can raise your mood and remind you that, even in tough moments, there are good things all around you.

List five things that you're grateful for: people, places, things; any positive experiences that occurred in the past or are happening right now. Describe in detail how they've influenced your life.

Though life can sometimes feel like a messy muddle, when you cultivate compassion for yourself, you can learn to trust that clarity will eventually arrive. Then you can begin to feel the effects of your daily gratitude and appreciation practice. Let's begin by exploring a moment of gratitude and joy.

What are one or two recent moments of happiness in your life?

_____

_____

_____

_____

_____

_____

Describe the situation(s), and anyone else involved. Share the specific feelings you had for yourself and others in this moment.

_____

_____

_____

_____

_____

_____

_____

Perhaps you aren't super excited about everything in your life in this moment. Can you still choose to look at yourself and your past through a lens of love, appreciation, and, most importantly, self-compassion? Everything that you've been through is part of your journey and has made you the unique person that you are. Remember, you can't control what happens to you, but you can control your response.

What is something you need to forgive yourself for?

_____

_____

_____

_____

_____

What is a lesson that has been difficult but important for you to learn from this experience?

_____

_____

_____

_____

_____

Think about a recent time in your life when you felt like a beginner. Maybe you decided to try a creative writing workshop or dance class, or tried your hand at a new sport or hobby. Why did you decide to take a risk and try something new? Were you successful? Did you fail?

How did the experience influence your decisions today? How did this new activity confirm or shift your perspective of what you are capable of doing and trying?

The relationships you choose to invest time into can reveal a lot about your values and priorities. For example, if you're drawn to active, adventurous friends, it's likely you're an active person. Think of a relationship in your life, past or present, that has changed you for the better. What about your life or perspective on life changed because of this relationship?

Exploring new surroundings is all about educating yourself and taking thoughtful risks. This is particularly true if you find yourself in a foreign country where you don't speak the language. Think of a time you traveled somewhere new—a new country, city, or even somewhere new in your current town. Remember how you felt as you took in the new sights, sounds, and smells.

Write about the experience as if you were sharing the details with a friend who had never been there before.

It's fair to say that trying something new or outside of your comfort zone can be scary. Sometimes the activity is truly terrifying, like bungee jumping. Other activities can be nerve-wracking but exciting, like starting a new job. Think about a time when you were scared to do something, but a part of you decided to do it anyway.

Describe the moment you felt the shift into, "I am doing this!"

What did you gain as a result of taking the leap?

When you were younger, maybe you loved to choreograph dances with your friends in the backyard or create elaborate dramas with your dolls or action figures. Whatever it was, you did it not to please anyone, but because you were following your inner joy. What activities did you love when you were younger, simply for the joy they brought into your life?

Choose one of those favorite activities. Write about it. Think about how you can bring it into your life in some small way today.

Who was your childhood best friend, or a group of friends that you spent a lot of time with when you were younger? Think about some of the fun things you used to like to do together. How did those experiences make you feel?

So much of who you are is a quilt of memories that you created with your family. Even if some parts (or many parts) of your childhood weren't amazing or even good, is there something that stands out as a good season or moment? What is one favorite memory of your family?

Describe it in as much detail as you can, as if you were telling the story to a friend.

Every time you experience or celebrate a proud personal moment, you build more self-worth and confidence. Think about a time from your past when you were proud of what you were able to attempt or accomplish, even though it was challenging.

How did it make you feel? What emotions do you recall from the experience? How does that make you feel today?

It can be hard to tell how much you've grown—until you're in a situation that would have previously been difficult for you, but that you can now see from a new perspective. Acknowledging your personal growth can help you keep going on days that feel more messy than magical.

How have you grown in the past year? Have you been more patient with your kids? Or maybe you've been journaling about your feelings so that you have a better understanding of yourself and your choices.

Write about specific habits and changes you have made. And remember—nothing is too small!

Sometimes our goals get sidetracked because we lose energy, get distracted, or life happens and moves us away from that goal. Sometimes you simply outgrow the goal because life has changed, and you now want different things.

What is a past or recent goal that you have not completed?

_____

_____

_____

_____

_____

Is this something you still want to work toward? Or are you ready to release this goal and make room for new ideas and inspiration?

_____

_____

_____

_____

_____

_____

It's important to find joy in your relationships—but most important to find it in the one you have with yourself. Increase that joy by writing a love letter to yourself.

It may feel awkward at first, and that's totally normal. It may help to imagine yourself at a different point in your life and look compassionately upon who you were and who you have become.

It can help to start your sentences with:

I love how you . . .

I appreciate you for . . .

I see how you try to . . .

You may have heard the saying "What doesn't kill you makes you stronger."

As difficult and painful as some life situations can be, you can build resilience through adversity if you take the time to acknowledge and process your emotions along the way.

Describe an experience that was painful at the time, but made you a stronger person.

"Mirror Work," developed by the late spiritual teacher Louise Hay, is a technique designed to help you get in touch with your inner self, and engage in self-love, self-care, and more meaningful relationships with others. By looking into the mirror and gently talking to yourself, you can foster a more compassionate, loving, and forgiving relationship with yourself.

Stand in front of the mirror and set a timer for five minutes.

You can choose to say something like, "I see you and I love you." Or you can say whatever kind and loving words come to you. You can also simply smile at yourself without saying or doing anything, and simply look into your own eyes until the timer is up.

When you're done, take a few minutes to write about your experience below.

We all make mistakes and fail miserably at different stages of our lives. These mistakes and failures are totally normal. Unfortunately, because your teenage years are a time to figure out who you are, and what you do and do not like, they are often riddled with mistakes.

Think about a time in your teens when you made a mistake that you wish you could undo.

What happened? And what would your current, wiser self say to your younger self?

Your home is a living scrapbook of your memories, experiences, and other things that make up your life. Walk around your home and look for an item that brings back good memories. Hold this item, if possible, and tap into the associated memories. Once you feel filled with the love and positive past images, take a few minutes to reflect on and share the memory below. If you know someone who would like to hear this memory, share it with them as well.

Life's best moments aren't always planned for. In fact, these surprises can sometimes seem pretty inconvenient at first. But sometimes cancelled social plans lead to a wonderful evening of self-care, or a job loss turns into an incredible opportunity to start your own business.

What unexpected event or situation ended up being a gift or growth opportunity in your life?

Music is a universal language of joy, emotions, and ceremony. In fact, you can simply hear a song that you used to listen to years ago, and it will conjure memories of that time in your life.

What types of music or songs do you associate with a past happy period in your life?

Set your timer for five to ten minutes. Choose one song that feels sad and one that brings up happier emotions. Listen to each song and pay attention to the emotions you are experiencing. Reflect on the different feelings you experience with each song.

"When I started counting my blessings,

my whole life turned around."

—WILLIE NELSON

Close your eyes, put your hand on your heart, and slowly repeat this three times: "I recognize every blessing, no matter how small."

"Courage starts with showing up

and letting ourselves be seen."

—BRENÉ BROWN

# See the World Anew

Fear is here to keep you out of harm's way. But when fear becomes a barrier to new adventures, new experiences, and a life that is fulfilling in ways you may not plan for, it may be time to take a closer look. In this section, you will find exercises and prompts to help you tune into and recognize your inner guidance. You will also explore how fear can be a friend and help you learn more about yourself. By investigating your fears, you will also foster the courage to discover new adventures.

The confidence to try something new can come from remembering your wins. Make a list of at least five wins you've had over the last decade—an amazing presentation that led to a job promotion, the awesome home renovation you did completely on your own, the time you helped your kid make a decision that helped deeply enrich their life—and share how you felt after each one.

You have a very wise inner guidance system which helps you steer clear of dangerous situations. It's this instinct that tells you to step away from the edge of a slippery cliff, or slow down at the yellow light to avoid a fender bender (or worse). Learning to listen to this inner guidance system and knowing when to heed its advice—or ignore it—is key to finding your inner magic again. What is something that you've been wanting to do, but have been too scared to try?

When it comes to trying new things or challenging yourself to do something way outside your normal routine, can you decide to make your fear into your friend?

What is one change that you've been thinking about for a while now, but that seems so overwhelming that you don't know where to begin?

_____

_____

_____

_____

_____

_____

What is one small step you can take in the direction of this change?

_____

_____

_____

_____

_____

_____

Understanding how your body reacts to fear is important to recognize—that way, you can begin to notice the physical signs and keep them in perspective. When you see a dark alley your mind and body take appropriate steps to keep you safe, yet that feeling of fear when it is time to speak publicly may keep you away from doing something meaningful.

Think of the last time you were scared to try something new. Close your eyes and really feel that experience. When you feel fearful, what happens within your body? Do you get hot and perspire? Does your pulse speed up? Does your stomach tighten? Share below.

Sometimes the things that scare you can also turn into new adventures, or new opportunities to experience life or yourself in a new way. Think back to something fun or new that you want to do in the near future—something that scares you when you think about it, but there is a part of you that is also a bit excited. Ask yourself the following questions:

What is the worst thing that can happen?

_____

_____

_____

_____

_____

_____

What is the best thing that can happen?

_____

_____

_____

_____

_____

_____

_____

Every experience has something to teach you. From the wins and successes to the failures and missteps, when you look back now, you can see that each situation in your life has brought you wisdom. The more you trust that you will either learn or grow from everything, the more willing you might be to take a risk, even a small one.

What is a key life lesson that you were only able to learn through a failure or misstep?

There are people in your life who may be doing things or living in a way that you admire and want for yourself. It can be easy to compare yourself to them and feel badly. But there is another way that you can see this type of situation: these people can be a mirror for you and for your desires. They can show you what is possible by making decisions or living in a way that you admire.

Think about who you admire for their courage, and why. Write down your reflections below.

It's important to stop and honor the ways you have already grown and the ways you continue to choose to be your authentic self every day, even if they are small. This includes acknowledging the many ways you are already living in a courageous way. Complete the following sentences:

I feel fear in my body or hear fearful thoughts in my mind when I . . .

<br>

When I notice the fear in my mind or in my body, I show courage by choosing to . . .

Paying too much attention to the opinions of others can make you doubt your own instincts and intuition. But while they may have the best intentions for you, you are the only one who can truly know what is right for you. Take a moment and think about an area of your life where you've been too worried about other people's opinions.

How has this worry held you back?

_____

_____

_____

_____

_____

_____

_____

_____

_____

_____

_____

_____

What is possible in your life when you drop all preconceived notions and tune out other people's opinions? Before you answer the following questions, close your eyes, take a few deep breaths, and allow a smile to emerge onto your face. Once you're centered in your innate, inner joy, finish the following sentences:

I'd like to be really good at . . .

_____

_____

_____

If I had all the time and money in the world, I would . . .

_____

_____

_____

I'm really curious about . . .

_____

_____

_____

There are things you do every single day—like brushing your teeth and making coffee—that you don't have to think about as you do them; they're simply habits. Good things can come out of being efficient and streamlining aspects of your life. But over time, habits can also lead you to become stuck in a rut. You can break out of this rut by either doing something completely new, or doing something you've always done, but in a new way.

What is one habit that is no longer serving you?

What is a new habit that you would like to implement?

When you choose to ignite your magic and live authentically, you also get to define life on your terms. This includes deciding what "courage" and "fear" mean to you. Something that is courageous to one person can feel normal to another.

What does the word "courage" mean to you?

_____

_____

_____

_____

_____

How will you lean into living with courage each day?

_____

_____

_____

_____

_____

_____

What if your fear were a person or animal? What would they look like? Describe the physical details of your fear. Be sure to give it a name. This can help you speak directly to your fear in the moments when you need to get clarity and move into courage.

The more you know about what scares you and why, the more you can see that you stay stuck in fear merely because of the "story" of what may happen. Consider the following:

Fear, what do you want me to know about this situation?

_____

_____

Fear, what do I need to remember about myself that could help me move forward?

_____

_____

Fear, what are you trying to protect me from?

_____

_____

Fear, what help or support can I ask for that would make you feel better about this situation?

_____

_____

What if your inner courage were a person or animal? What would they look like? Describe the physical details of your courage. Be sure to give it a name. This can help you speak directly to your courageous self when you need to get clarity and move into something new.

One of the ways you can begin to gently shift your life toward magic and fulfillment is by getting to know yourself now, as well as your past selves. You've grown and changed over the years, and now it's time to honor and acknowledge some of those changes, so that you can make mindful choices for yourself each day. Start by answering the following questions:

What drains your energy and exhausts you?

_____

_____

_____

What makes you feel alive with joy?

_____

_____

_____

What makes you feel fulfilled?

_____

_____

_____

Living a magical life as your most authentic self means making those tiny commitments in each area of your life. This is how you turn that big ocean liner—one decision at a time. Decisions made without clear commitments can leave you feeling frustrated, because you know how you want to feel but are not clear on what you want to do.

It's time to make a tiny commitment to the most important areas of your life. Remember, you can learn to feel the fear and do it anyway.

Finish the following sentence:

This week, I will create a tiny change in my life by . . .

| | |
|---|---|
| **EXAMPLE: MORNING ROUTINE** | I commit to waking up five to ten minutes early this week to move my body, journal, and meditate, so that I can start my day with positive energy and intention. |
| **MORNING ROUTINE** | |
| **HEALTH & WELLNESS** | |
| **CREATIVITY** | |
| **RELATIONSHIPS** | |
| **ONE THING THAT EXCITES AND SCARES ME** | |

True change doesn't happen in one day; rather, it comes from a series of small, honest choices that you make to honor yourself. Living an authentic life, full of magic and possibility, starts with getting to know yourself and being honest about what you want, need, and choose every day.

How are you becoming more honest about yourself and your life?

_____

_____

_____

_____

_____

What needs, wants, and desires are you ready to claim and create for yourself now?

_____

_____

_____

_____

_____

_____

When a dog or cat gets scared, you can see them shake their entire body. When the fear passes, they simply move on with their day. When you feel fear, tension, or just want to elevate your mood, you can "shake it off" too.

Put on your favorite music and, without overthinking it, start moving your hands as if you were shaking off some water.

Continue moving by shrugging your shoulders, gently bouncing them up and down.

You can move your body in any way that feels good to you.

Notice how you feel before and after.

Just like Wonder Woman puts on her tiara and gold cuffs before she goes out to fight crime, what you wear has an effect on how you feel and what you do. Get curious about what colors and outfits make you feel courageous or powerful.

What do you wear when you feel bold, powerful, and like the most courageous risk-taking, can't-get-it-wrong version of yourself?

If there is nothing you currently wear that makes you feel empowered, imagine what it could be and write out a list. (For example, a red scarf, or a sweater in the most beautiful shade of your favorite color.)

"Nothing in life is to be feared,

it is only to be understood.

Now is the time to understand

more, so that we may fear less."

—MARIE CURIE

Close your eyes, put your hand on your heart, and slowly repeat this three times:
"I easily access my inner courage whenever it is required, and listen well to the signals of my body."

"Leap, and the net will appear."

—JOHN BURROUGHS

# Light Your Creative Fire

There are some things in life that we simply have no control over, and some decisions we make that are more practical than magical. And though life may not have gone as planned, every step, misstep, and unexpected opportunity has something to teach you about yourself.

By doing the work in this *Ignite Your Magic* journal, you are learning to glean wisdom from your past and claim the magic in your future, as well as focus on what matters most to you now. How do you discover what matters most? Use the following exercises and prompts to become an observer of your own life.

When you have too many thoughts swirling around, writing can help you get some of them out and increase clarity. Take a few minutes now to sit quietly and do some deep, slow breathing. When your mind wanders, simply come back to your breath.

Now, set your timer for five minutes or more, and write down the first things that you think of. No need to edit, simply let the words flow without revision. Trust yourself to just keep going. If you're having trouble getting started, write about the things you can hear or see in this moment.

From the moment you wake up, it's easy to get swept up in the momentum of other people's needs. What would it look like to start your morning with some intentional time to fill your own cup and set the tone for your entire day? Using my Good-Better-Best model, come up with new morning routines.

| GOOD (5–15 MINUTES) | BETTER (15–30 MINUTES) | BEST (60+ MINUTES) |
|---|---|---|
| *Example: Do yoga stretches and write down my intention for the day.* | *Example: Dance to one or two songs, meditate for five minutes, and write out my thoughts for the day in my journal.* | *Example: Take a bath, do yoga stretches, and light a candle and meditate. Journal with colored pencils and take time to really nourish my body, mind, and soul by asking my inner self what I need most now.* |
|  |  |  |

One of the things that can hold you back from making authentic choices is listening to the opinions of others around you. Think about times in your life where the opinions of others swayed your decisions—maybe they chose the college you attended, the kinds of clothing you wore, or the career you chose. This isn't about blame; this is about recognizing where you can take back your own power and make choices that feel good to you.

Write out a few things that you would like to begin doing your own way, regardless of what others may think.

With all of life's distractions, staying present can be a struggle. One way to connect with yourself, your intuition, and your creativity is to practice being present to the power of now. The best way to get into the present moment is to focus on your breath.

Write yourself a note to keep with you, or schedule a reminder on your phone that will pop up every hour, with the words "Stop now and take three slow breaths." This hourly cue will remind you to breathe and help you live in the present, which is where inspiration resides.

Using your imagination can help you see yourself in a new way, as well as help you stay in the present moment. Start by thinking about any animals in nature that you loved when you were a child.

What is one animal that you liked? If you were that animal, how would you act in your natural habitat?

Describe the animal and the attributes and characteristics that you would have if you were that animal.

Think back to when you were a kid in school. Did you learn that there was a right and wrong way to draw or to write stories? Maybe a teacher told you that you were doing it all wrong. Let's practice busting some of those old rules now. Write a short poem or story about something you can see in your environment right now. Choose the first thing that catches your attention. There are no rules. It doesn't even have to rhyme.

As an adult, it's so easy to fall into a pattern of "taking care of business" that you can forget to slow down, smile, play, and get messy. Take a moment now and think about something that you love to do, but never seem to find time for. It could be doing a puzzle or trying out a new recipe. Write out a list of five things that you want to make time for. Then choose one that you can go and do today.

Life is filled with wrong turns. But more often than not, those turns take you to exactly where you need to be. The more you can learn to trust the detours, the more open you become to releasing the idea of how things should be, and feeling the magic of how things could be. Write about a time you took a wrong turn, showed up late, or made what seemed like an error—only to find that it led you to something good—or even better than you imagined.

When you're getting things done and taking care of other people, life can fall into a mundane-feeling pattern. Sometimes weeks, months, and even years can go by, and it can feel like your life is missing that spark of magic and adventure.

Have you fallen into a day-to-day rut in your life? Imagine if you could change a few things up to add some joy and play.

Imagine that you have a magic wand for a day. What would you do with your powers? What would you change or create in your life? Have fun imagining!

Your creative endeavors are like planting a seed in the ground and trusting that the flower will bloom when it's ready. As you start a new creative endeavor, you may not feel skilled enough or see a dramatic result right away, but you know that growth is happening in its own time.

What is one creative skill that you would like to begin or develop?

As a kid, when you watched the clouds go by, your mind naturally saw animals and objects in them. This kind of free time for your mind can stimulate many creative ideas, realizations, and aha moments. Right now, whether you are outside or need to find a window, set a timer for five minutes and then simply look out and notice the sky above.

When the timer goes off, write about what you noticed and experienced, as well as any ideas that percolated for you.

Allowing yourself to be present, playful, and create just for fun can open up new ways of seeing in your life. Originally created by Bob McKim of the Stanford Design Program, the 30 Circles Exercise—and specifically, this variation on it—can get you out of your logical mind and into playful possibility.

Set a timer for three minutes. Then, using just one pencil, color in, draw on, and decorate as many squares in the grid below as possible—with the aim being quantity, not quality. Your one goal is to fill as many circles as possible. The idea behind the 30 Circles is to stop yourself from self-censoring.

The things that you notice about your days can tell you a lot about what is important to you. This includes the things you choose to take a picture of. Look through the most recent pictures that you've taken with your smartphone or camera. Scan through and find one that makes you feel joyful, then think of a whole story based on the picture.

Write out the story of that picture and day, as if you were sharing the story with a dear friend.

Think about an era in history that you would enjoy living in or exploring. It could be the Roaring Twenties, the neon 1980s, or another time entirely. If you could visit for a day, where would you go and why? Write about traveling back in time, and what a day in that time might be like for you.

Doodling is such a great way to get out of your head and give yourself permission to create something just for fun, with zero pressure to be an "artist."

Set a timer for five to ten minutes and just let your pen or pencil lead the way. After you're done, write down any thoughts, inspiration, or reflections that came up during your doodling time.

Your morning routine starts the night before. This means that you set yourself up for a mindful morning routine when you pay attention to your nighttime routine. Think about some ways that you can make your bedroom and nighttime routine more pleasant for yourself—a comfy pillow, low lights, relaxing color on the walls. What feels right to you? Make a list of a few ways that you could easily make your bedtime routine more pleasant and peaceful.

Stretching yourself, even if it's simply reading a book in a new genre, can bring about new perspectives, inspire creativity, and open new ways of seeing the world.

Think of a type of book you don't normally read—say, a mystery novel, if you usually only read nonfiction. Then commit to reading one book in this genre that is outside your comfort zone.

Believing that you have to struggle before you become good at anything can block your creativity. Another perspective is that you were born with an innate set of talents that come easily to you. For example, maybe math is a snap for you, but drawing isn't. Or you have a friend who is a naturally talented artist, but has to struggle with math.

What is something that comes to you so easily that others may see as an incredible skill? Jot down some ideas below and reflect on how you can do more of what comes easy.

Creativity can take on many forms. For one person, it might be gardening; for another, it may look like grabbing some markers or colored pens and drawing or doodling while listening to their favorite soundtrack. There are truly no rules when it comes to creative expression.

Think about three things that sound like fun right now—things you'd enjoy just for the fun of creating. Now choose one and go do it.

It's okay to let go of old dreams to make way for new ones. When you think about your own life from the perspective of your 15-year-old self, what did you envision your future might look like? Did you end up following the path you laid out for yourself? Or did life throw you some curveballs?

Take a moment right now and write about what you thought your adult life would look like when you were 15. Did it turn out that way? How do you feel about that?

_____

_____

_____

_____

_____

_____

_____

_____

_____

_____

_____

Moving your body is a great creative outlet. And getting out of your typical movement patterns can inspire new ideas. Put on a song you love, one with a strong beat, and move in a way that feels good, but is not the way that you would normally dance to music. Take up space and have fun.

A change of scenery can do wonders to stir up new perspectives and new energy. Take a distraction-free walk around your neighborhood or somewhere else that you go frequently.

Set an intention to notice at least three new things that you haven't seen before.

"Creativity is not just for artists.

It's for businesspeople looking for

a new way to close a sale; it's for

engineers trying to solve a problem;

it's for parents who want their children

to see the world in more than one way."

—TWYLA THARP

Close your eyes, put your hand on your heart, and slowly repeat this three times: "I am ready to lovingly share my authentic voice and expression."

"I would rather walk with a friend in

the dark, than alone in the light."

—HELEN KELLER

# Build Community That Sparks Joy

Human beings are designed to be social and in community. A community can be a small group of two or three friends, or a large network of people that you know through a shared interest or organization. Community can be there for you when times are tough and rejoice with you in times of celebration. And you can do the same for those in your community.

Regardless of the size of your community, taking time to show up and nourish those connections can have a profound, positive impact on your life and the lives of others.

When you're a kid, the people around you tend to be whoever is in your class or lives in your neighborhood. As you get older, you can have more control over the people you choose to spend time with. You also get to choose to create connections with people who support and accept you, as well as encourage you to be who you really are. Think about the people that you tend to be in contact with most often.

Who are the people that inspire you, or with whom you have the most positive overall interactions?

_____

_____

_____

_____

_____

Who are the people who tend to be more discouraging when you have new ideas?

_____

_____

_____

_____

_____

When you explore and express your authentic self (as you're doing in these journal pages), the people around you may begin to react differently, as well. Some may be inspired by your changes, while others may need some time to adjust.

Take this opportunity to claim the kind of friendships you want to cultivate and nurture in your life.

Complete the following statements:

A true friend is . . .

_____

_____

_____

_____

_____

The way I can be a true friend is . . .

_____

_____

_____

_____

_____

Connecting with people who have great energy will inspire you. Seek out role models who live as their most authentic selves. These can be people you know personally, or people whom you've read about, or know from their work in the world. It can even include people from history whose life and accomplishments stand out to you.

Who are three people you admire? What specific qualities about them stand out to you?

Even if you want to make new friends or nurture existing relationships, there can be roadblocks—like not making enough time to cultivate these new relationships, or worrying that your new friends will only like you if you think exactly like them. What obstacles or stresses have you felt in the past when trying to make new friends? What steps can you take now to change those patterns?

What you focus your attention on expands. You can use this truth to nourish your friendships by taking the time to acknowledge the things that you appreciate about your friends and the connections you share.

What are some qualities your friends have that you truly appreciate? Write a paragraph for each person, praising these qualities and the relationship. When you're finished, make sure to let them know how much you appreciate these qualities—and their friendship.

Children rarely overthink friendships or hold grudges. They simply enjoy being together and having fun. We can learn a lot from children and the easy way they approach new friendships.

Can you think of the earliest friend you made? What drew you to them?

Authentic friendships and community can help you live in a richer and more aligned way. You can create more conscious connections by getting clear on what you want more of in your friendships—and what you want less of. Visualize the ideal way you want to live your life, and then answer these questions from that perspective.

What would it feel amazing to have more of when it comes to friendships and community?

What would it feel freeing to have less of when it comes to friendships and community?

Finding connections and a community where you are accepted and encouraged to be your true self is a gift. Think of a time in your life, either now or in the past, when you truly felt like you belonged. Describe this community and the qualities that gave you a sense of welcome and belonging.

You can create deeper friendships by being the kind of friend that you want to have. In all friendships, it's important to give and to receive. Sometimes a tiny action of appreciation, like a letter, text, or phone call sharing your gratitude for your friend, can go a long way in creating a deeper connection.

Make a list of three to five relationships in your life that are important to you. Then list out some small action you can take to send a little love and attention to each person.

Feeling a sense of belonging makes you stronger and more resilient, because you know that no matter what happens, you have a network of support to rely on. Think about some of the natural communities that you are already part of—your neighborhood, your coworkers at your job, your family members, or any other group that you are part of. Write about one connection that you would like to spend more time and energy developing, and brainstorm a few ways you can do so.

"Don't ask yourself what the world needs; ask yourself what makes you come alive. And then go and do that. Because what the world needs is people who have come alive."

—HOWARD THURMAN

It may sound counterintuitive, but the more you allow yourself to be selfish and make time for what feels joyful to you, the more you actually give others permission to find their own inner joy. Pretty cool, right? Think about the activities or situations that make you feel alive and joyful.

Define what being "alive" means to you. Set a timer and write for at least 10 minutes.

Liking all of yourself is about learning to have self-worth and self-value. Consciously choosing how you want to show up begins with learning to fully accept yourself—even the things that feel difficult to like. If you haven't done this before, it can feel a bit awkward to make a list of things you like about yourself, but stay with it!

What do people like about you? Are these the same things you like about yourself?

_____

_____

_____

_____

_____

If not, what are the things you like about yourself?

_____

_____

_____

_____

_____

The more you spend time learning about yourself, the more authentic your interactions with others will be. Think about the activities that make you feel most like yourself. Set the timer for five minutes and keep writing the entire time. Invite yourself to go beyond the obvious answers.

I feel most like myself when I . . .

Generosity is a staple value of a well-tended community. Each community has its own ideas about how to give time, energy, or material things within that context. How generous are you?

Rate yourself on a scale from 0 to 5 for the following statements, and if there is a score that does not feel generous to you, ask yourself what you can do to take it up to the next level.

I am generous with my time.

I am generous with my appreciation.

I am generous with my stuff.

I am generous with my money.

Feeling like you have to do everything yourself can create stress in your life and make you feel unsupported. What is one area of your life or work where you feel drained—an area where it would feel really good to ask for support? Make a plan for how to get that support. For instance, instead of doing everything yourself, is there an area where you can delegate some household chores?

There are so many ways that you can help and support yourself and those around you. Make a list of skills that you could use to help someone else in your life.

There are qualities that you may want to seek out as you build your close connections. You may want to connect with people who have qualities like emotional availability, listening skills, a sense of humor, an attitude of gratitude, and a zest for life. Think about the best qualities from past relationships, as well as qualities that you wished for but were absent.

What are some important qualities or values that you want to look for when creating supportive relationships in your life?

Think of the people who are important to you—family or friends. Reflect on how they affect your life and how you feel when you spend time with them. With these thoughts in mind, set a timer for five minutes and finish the following sentences.

I am grateful for ................................................................................................................................

Specifically, I appreciate ....................................................................................................

................................................................................................................................................

................................................................................................................................................

................................................................................................................................................

Staying consistent and true to your own needs—even when it feels difficult to do so—matters. Take a look at your values list from the previous prompt, and think about each value and how you can make it a priority in your life.

Write about your intentions to stay true to your values around friendship and community.

Remember how much fun it was to receive a handwritten letter or postcard in the mail? You can still be a part of that fun. Write cards or letters to three people who have touched your life in some way, letting them know the effect their actions had on you.

Creating personal boundaries can help you prioritize your values—and prevent other people from treating you in ways that conflict with what's important to you. Writing out your values can help you make them more of a priority in your life. Make a list of the top five most important things in your life—they could be family, health, freedom, creativity, compassion, generosity, integrity, play, success, learning, or anything else.

Think about a club or group that you might like to be a part of. Maybe it's a book club. Or maybe you'd love to invite a few friends to hike with you regularly. Make a list of three to five clubs or groups that you would like to be part of. Once you have written the list, choose one that feels most fun for you, and take a tiny risk by reaching out to a few new or existing friends and asking them to join you.

Imagine coming home and finding a sweet little gift at your front door. Finding a little something special can create feelings of happiness, connectedness, and being seen. Brainstorm a list of ways you can share a little gift with a neighbor, a coworker, or even someone who lives in your home. It can be super simple—a small, handwritten note with a hand-picked flower, or a small bag of homemade cookies. Make sure to give your gift within a week.

Close your eyes, put your hand on your heart, and slowly repeat this three times: "The more I love and honor myself and my gifts, the more easily I attract wonderful, positive people into my life."

"Rule of thumb: The more important

a call to action is to our soul's evolution,

the more resistance we will feel toward

pursuing it."

—STEVEN PRESSFIELD,
*The Art of War*

# Nurture Your Magic and Watch It Grow

This section is about moving forward on your journey with magic and joy, and staying true to that unique, magical person you have become. It's time to focus your attention on nourishing yourself and building a daily practice that nurtures your inner magic and helps you create a life you love.

A mantra is a meaningful word or phrase that you repeat to yourself to help you focus and feel present, and to shut down any negativity. One of the most powerful ways to declare your magic is through a daily mantra you repeat to yourself or say out loud.

A mantra should be meaningful to you and easy to remember. For example:

Life is unfolding in my favor, even when it seems bumpy.

I am grateful for the life I have while pursuing the life I desire.

I am igniting magic in my life.

Now write your own mantra.

Sometimes your authentic self can be quite different from the practical part of you that handles adult responsibilities. What did you discover about yourself while using this journal that most surprised you?

The best way to happily show up for the important people in your life is to show up for yourself. For example, you could take one morning each week to do something just for you. How will you continue to nourish your most authentic self each week?

Brainstorm a list of 10 tiny ways you can love and nourish yourself this week, then put them on your calendar.

1. ......................................................................................................................

2. ......................................................................................................................

3. ......................................................................................................................

4. ......................................................................................................................

5. ......................................................................................................................

6. ......................................................................................................................

7. ......................................................................................................................

8. ......................................................................................................................

9. ......................................................................................................................

10. ....................................................................................................................

......................................................................................................................

......................................................................................................................

......................................................................................................................

......................................................................................................................

Practicing saying no in a kind and loving way can help you avoid saying yes out of habit or fear of disappointing someone else. Think about a situation in your life where you would like to say no to a request of your time. Brainstorm a few ways that you can gracefully decline an invitation—for example, "Thank you for asking, but this doesn't work for me at this time."

To stay on your magical path, create a vision of your life that excites you, is meaningful, is manageable, and that you'll look forward to six months from now.

Where do you see yourself?

_____

_____

_____

_____

How are you spending your days?

_____

_____

_____

_____

What changes have you happily made in your life?

_____

_____

_____

_____

"I believe that everyone chooses how to approach life. If you're proactive, you focus on preparing. If you're reactive, you end up focusing on repairing."

—JOHN C. MAXWELL

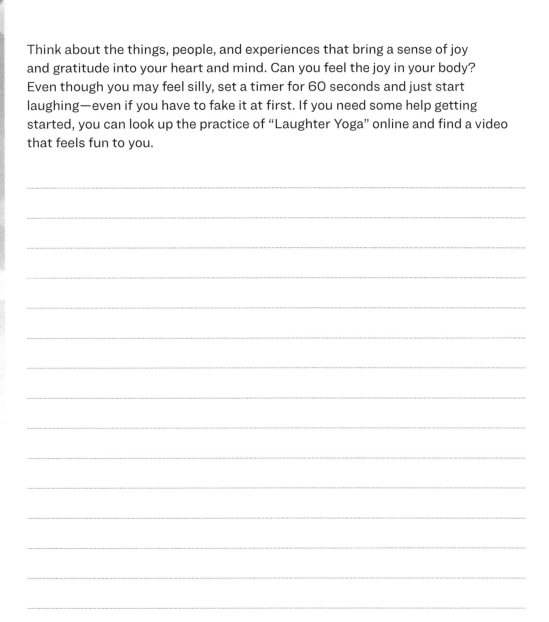

Think about the things, people, and experiences that bring a sense of joy and gratitude into your heart and mind. Can you feel the joy in your body? Even though you may feel silly, set a timer for 60 seconds and just start laughing—even if you have to fake it at first. If you need some help getting started, you can look up the practice of "Laughter Yoga" online and find a video that feels fun to you.

Sometimes the changes you make in your life are so tiny and incremental that it's hard to feel like anything has really changed. But realizing that it has could be as simple as noticing that you have more patience in frustrating situations, or a new habit that now feels like it is second nature. What changes or shifts have you noticed in yourself or your life over the last few months that now feel natural for you?

The process of asking powerful questions and living your most magical life can help you shed what no longer serves you. It can also shift your identity in positive ways. You have gained beautiful insights and inner clarity. The process is not always pretty, but in doing this, you can learn to trust and believe in your own magic.

How will I carry the lessons I learned from this journey forward in my life?

By letting go of .........................................................................................................

.........................................................................................................................

.........................................................................................................................

.........................................................................................................................

.....................................................................................................................,

I create space for .......................................................................................................

.........................................................................................................................

.........................................................................................................................

.........................................................................................................................

......................................................................................................................

Fill out this "magic-libs" story with the most meaningful moments that you have had throughout this journaling journey.

Start here, and feel free to add your own twists and turns:

"Once upon a time there was a ........................... named ............................. .

........................... was very ..........................., ..........................., and ........................... .

...........................lived in ........................... with ........................... .

Each morning, ........................... set the intention to ........................... .

Their favorite thing about their life was ........................... .

Their least favorite thing was ........................... .

More than anything, they desired ........................... .

The only challenge was that ........................... .

One day, it was ..........................., when out of the blue ..........................."

Continue the story to completion.

_____

_____

_____

_____

_____

_____

The way you perceive fear and courage is a huge factor in your journey of growth and self-discovery. Bringing awareness to your thoughts, doubts, and fears can help lessen the power they hold over you. Think about the top doubts and/or fears you have about creating positive changes in your life. Write about your top three doubts and/or fears.

Having a role model can inspire, empower, and motivate you to keep moving toward your goals. Make a list of five individuals—it does not matter if they are famous, close to you personally, or somewhere in between—and exactly why you look up to them.

Yes, it's important to grow, learn, and find ways to feel like you are closer to living your values. But it's also important to remember that you are naturally able to help others just by being yourself. Whether you're helping a friend in need or helping out a neighbor, you have magic to share. Describe an instance when you helped someone else get closer to their goals or solve a problem, and how this made you feel afterward.

Staying healthy builds your mental resilience, is proven to prevent burnout, and can support long-term success in all areas of your life. Think about a wellness habit that you want to start and commit to everyday. It can be as simple as taking a short walk each day after lunch or dinner, or adding more variety to your veggie intake.

One of the ways you've explored igniting more magic in your life is by noticing how your surroundings affect your energy, your mood, and your overall experience of your life.

Think about any places that have made you feel amazing. For example, a space in your own home, a hotel room you may have visited, or a place in nature where you feel happy. Write about the spaces that make you feel most alive, and share some details about why you love those spaces.

Learning can be a lifelong goal, beyond formal education. With all of the resources available online, you can learn any topic or subject of interest to you—from illustration to yoga to voice lessons, there is no limit. What would you like to learn about? How will you go about doing this?

We are all born with the natural ability to be creative. Children have no rules about creativity—except the ones they hear from adults. It's time to make some messy magic.

Right now, think about your favorite flower or tree. Set the timer for five minutes and simply draw five versions of that flower using pencils, pens, or markers. Try not to overthink it and simply have fun. When the timer goes off, feel free to keep going.

"Inner guidance is heard like

soft music in the night by those

who have learned to listen."

—VERNON HOWARD

There are so many things that make you a unique person. From the way you see life to the way you connect with people to the way you create. There are no two people who are exactly the same, and those differences are a beautiful thing. Right now, close your eyes for one minute, and ask yourself, "What makes me unique?" After the minute is up, write down any image, word, or idea that came to you.

As you continue to move forward on your magical journey, you may begin to feel so good that you're tempted to try and simply forget about past mistakes. But mistakes rarely stay forgotten—instead, we have to work through them to move on from them. It's time to release the past and make space for more of your magic to bubble up into all areas of your life.

What is one past mistake that you are ready to release right now?

Is there someone in your community who is doing good work that might be going unnoticed? Perhaps it's a single parent who is working hard to give their children a good life, or the checkout clerk at your grocery store who always shows up to work with a smile to share.

Write a thank-you card to this person, specifically mentioning the way you notice and appreciate them. Share the card via mail or in-person delivery, and watch the magic sharing appreciation unfolds.

As you make changes in your life, you may outgrow things that once made you happy. You may be ready for new and different kinds of entertainment, and content to match your new ideas and intentions for life. What media and information sources can inspire and elevate you toward your magical self?

Nature is magical, not to mention very healing and soothing to your nervous system. Being in nature can help you get out of your busy mind and become present, which is where your inner magic lives. Bring this journal to a place you love in nature and set a timer to just observe for at least 10 minutes. Then journal or draw any insights that came up for you.

Being in a sacred space can help you ignite your magic. You can create sacred space in your own home. This can be a place where you meditate, journal, or simply find a moment of inner peace. Choose a space in your home—like a window-sill or nightstand—and organize it in a way that feels good to you. If you already have a sacred space, take a few minutes to dust it off, and add or remove anything that feels good to you at this moment.

Close your eyes, put your hand on your heart, and slowly repeat this three times: "Every moment in my life, I get to choose joy, I get to choose me, and I get to choose a new beginning."

"Trust yourself. Create the kind of self that you will be happy to live with all your life. Make the most of yourself by fanning the tiny, inner sparks of possibility into flames of achievement."

—GOLDA MEIR

# A Final Word

You are deserving of a life that lights you up.

You are worthy of living your heart's desire.

You are here to take up space and connect in ways that matter to you.

The more of yourself that you share, the more your life inspires those around you, simply by being the magical, authentic YOU that you are.

You are extraordinary.

You are magic!

You did it! Take a deep breath and know that you have done the good work to ignite your magic. You have given yourself the gift of stepping into a new way of being and experiencing your life. You've taken time for yourself to reflect on what matters most to you.

Now you get to choose your next step, and your next. It is my deepest hope that you have received some powerful insights and tools that you can keep coming back to time and time again.

May you be reminded of your own authentic magic each time you look in the mirror, meet a new challenge, or have a choice to make on your unique path. More than anything, stay gentle with yourself on this journey. Sometimes you will take a step back into old patterns. This is normal. You can love yourself through it, and choose a new way to show up each and every day.

I am so grateful that you chose this journey with me and with yourself. Until we meet again, may you remember, that:

It's the tiny, daily steps that change your life over time.

You can trust that by tending to your inner, magical self in small ways, you will be able to consciously navigate anything that comes your way with grace and authenticity.

xoxo

Elena

# Resources

## Podcasts

*Find Your Voice* with Allison Fallon

*The Mind Your Business Podcast* with James Wedmore

*Heroine* with Majo Molfino

and my podcast:

*Divinely Aligned Meditations & Musings* by Elena Lipson

## Books

*The Big Leap* by Gay Hendricks

*The Artist's Way* by Julia Cameron

*The Way of Integrity* by Martha Beck

## A Few Websites to Inspire Daily Magic

The Universe Talks by Mike Dooley: A wonderful way to connect with the magic of the universe.

tut.com

Alexandra Franzen, a multitalented writer who inspires me in countless ways.

AlexandraFranzen.com

# References

## Get to Know Yourself (Again)

Harvard Health Publishing. "Giving Thanks Can Make You Happier." November 22, 2011. health.harvard.edu/healthbeat/giving-thanks-can-make-you-happier.

Martin, Rod A. "Do Children Laugh Much More Often than Adults Do?" Association for Applied and Therapeutic Humor. 4/19/21 aath.memberclicks.net/do-children -laugh-much-more-often-than-adults-do.

Power, Rhett. "A Day of Rest: 23 Scientific Reasons It Works" Inc. January 1, 2017. inc.com/rhett-power/a-day-of-rest-12-scientific-reasons-it-works.html.

Stevens, Jenn. "My Magic Morning: An Easy 5-Step Spiritual Morning Routine." The Aligned Life. thealignedlife.co/my-magic-morning-an-easy-5-step-spiritual -morning-routine.

## Having Compassion and Gratitude for Your Journey

Hay, Louise. "What Is Mirror Work?" LouiseHay.com. 4/27/21 louisehay.com /what-is-mirror-work.

## Light Your Creative Fire

McKim, Bob. "Thirty Circles Exercise." In *Creative Confidence: Unleashing the Creative Potential Within Us All*, written by Tom Kelley and David Kelley. New York: Crown Business, 2013.

Stevens, Jenn. "My Magic Morning: An Easy 5-Step Spiritual Morning Routine." The Aligned Life. thealignedlife.co/my-magic-morning-an-easy-5-step-spiritual -morning-routine.

## Nurture Your Magic and Watch It Grow

Kataria, Madan. Laughter Yoga. Laughter Yoga International. laughteryoga.org.

# Acknowledgments

To my sweetest hubby and son, thank you for cooking the meals, walking the dogs, and letting me share the celebrations as I finished each section of this book.

To my dearest soul-bestie, you know who you are. Thank you for always speaking the truth to me and for me. You are a symbol of the highest integrity. May our friendship span three more decades and beyond.

To my sister, I thank you for always believing in my words and in my magic, especially in the moments when I couldn't see it for myself. To my mama, thank you for always being my biggest fan and supporting all of my twists and turns. I love you always.

To my editor, Carolyn Abate, thank you for holding my hand and guiding me on this journey. Your kindness, notes, and guidance helped me to craft something that I know will change lives.

To all of my clients, thank you for showing up and letting me share my magic.

And finally, and most importantly, to you my dear reader. Thank you for following your nudge to pick up this journal, and for being so willing to explore and share your magic. You are amazing!

Let's Connect:

instagram.com/elena_lipson

facebook.com/divineselfcarementor

# About the Author

ELENA LIPSON is a writer, speaker, intuitive mentor, and magic maker. Elena loves to help people connect with innate magic, so they never put joy, daily wealth, or happiness on hold.

Drawing on her experience as a corporate trainer, coach, and entrepreneur, Elena also guides her clients and students to design a life and work that are built on a foundation of self-care, intuition, and self-trust.

Elena grew up developing her street smarts and taste for delicious food in NYC. She now lives in the Pacific Northwest where you can find her making meals for friends, trying new restaurants, going hiking with her family, or paddling in the sparkly lake, weaving her way through all of the magic.